*Ruth Martindale*

# poems
## *from the*
### *heart*

# POEMS FROM THE HEART

*Trust in the Lord with all thine heart,
and lean not unto thine own
understanding; In all thy ways
acknowledge Him,
and He shall direct thy paths.*

Prov 3: 5, 6

Ruth Martindale

Second Printing
December, 1994

Copyright © 1994, FOCUS PUBLISHING INC.

All rights reserved. No part of this book my be reproduced by any means without written consent of the publisher except for brief quotes used in reviews written specifically for use in a magazine or newspaper.

Cover photograph - Shawn D. Winters

ISBN 1-885904-01-0

PRINTED IN THE UNITED STATES OF AMERICA
BY
FOCUS PUBLISHING
INCORPORATED
Bemidji, Minnesota

*To my son Jim, and
grandson Eric . . .*

*. . . and to the memory of
my husband Art and son David*

# Contents

| | | | |
|---|---|---|---|
| *Fluttering Wings* | 3 | *The Ladder Beside You* | 29 |
| *It's So Easy* | 4 | *How Much Time For Me?* | 30 |
| *Autumn Leaves* | 6 | *Not Without Him* | 31 |
| *Yearning* | 7 | *Just a Pilgrim* | 32 |
| *Broken Pieces* | 8 | *Perfect Peace* | 33 |
| *Do You Wonder?* | 9 | *Full of Joy* | 34 |
| *First Love* | 11 | *The Stranger* | 35 |
| *Another Christmas* | 12 | *WMBI* | 36 |
| *He Cares* | 13 | *The Adversary* | 38 |
| *I'll Be Waiting* | 14 | *A Teacher's Prayer* | 39 |
| *His Hands* | 15 | *God's Hand* | 41 |
| *I Care* | 16 | *He Was There* | 42 |
| *Arrival* | 17 | *Bookworm* | 44 |
| *His Star of Gold* | 19 | *Not Easy Being Green* | 45 |
| *Possessions* | 20 | *My Jim* | 47 |
| *The Master Potter* | 21 | *Father's Songs* | 48 |
| *My Message* | 22 | *A Rival* | 49 |
| *My Prayer* | 23 | *A Mother's Crusade* | 50 |
| *My Resurrection Day* | 24 | *Cloud of Grief* | 52 |
| *The Other Chapel* | 25 | *Still Flying* | 53 |
| *Troubled Waters* | 26 | *Heavenly Passport* | 54 |
| *Unrest* | 27 | *Waiting Room* | 55 |
| *Only Leaves* | 28 | | |

***From the author....***

*These poems were written over a period of many years after accepting Christ as my Saviour as a teenager. They are a personal testimony to His love and faithfulness to me through times of joy and times of great sorrow. I share them in the hope that these poems from my heart will touch your heart.*

## Fluttering Wings

*A butterfly held captive
In a young lad's little hands
Will vainly flutter wings
To escape its earthly bands.*

*And the lad will cup his hands
Like a globe around his prize
To protect the delicate wings
As the anxious fluttering dies.*

*And I, so oft perturbed
By hopes still unfulfilled,
Am cradled in His hands
Until my fluttering wings are stilled!*

*Lord, when I'm overwhelmed
By some sorrow this life brings,
Oh, take me in Your hands
And still my fluttering wings!*

*When I'm hurting deep within -
When my soul no longer sings,
Lord, wrap your arms around me
And still my fluttering wings!*

## It's So Easy

When abundant good health is my portion,
I find it so easy to say,
I'll trust Thee in sickness and health, Lord,
Just send what Thou will 'long my way.

But oh, when Thou sendest affliction
And my body's in pain and so weak,
That's when I really trust Thee
If in it Thy purpose I seek.

It's so easy to trust Thee, dear Lord,
To give me my daily bread
When the savings are there in the bank
And provision for days far ahead.

But oh, when the savings are gone
And the larder starts growing bare,
That's when I really trust Thee
If I commit it to Thee, Lord, in prayer.

It's so easy to say I need no one,
Only Thee, precious Lord, only Thee,
When my family and friends are around me
And I'm content as a person can be.

But oh, when you take them away, Lord,
And there is no one but Thee,
That's when I'll really prove
How sufficient Thy grace is for me.

*It's so easy to say I won't fear
The valley of the shadow of death
When the valley seems far in the distance
And I'm blessed with life-giving breath.*

*But when the day finally comes, Lord,
That the river of death I must ford,
It's then that I'll know what it means
To walk home hand in hand with my Lord!*

## Autumn Leaves

*How beautiful the tree had been -
Resplendent in autumn dress,
Now becoming gaunt and bare,
Each day its foliage less.*

*How quickly some of the golden leaves
Flow down with effortless ease,
While others, in no haste to part,
Wait for the autumn breeze.*

*And then there are the final few
Who hold on tenaciously,
As if they cannot bear at all
To leave the mother tree.*

*Am I not like the resisting leaf,
Reluctant to have the Lord sever
His child from things too deeply loved
And wanting possession forever?*

*Keep me from holding on like the leaf
That resists floating down to the sod -
Unclasp hands that too tightly hold on,
Lord, help me "let go and let God!"*

## Yearning

*Ever to yearn for my Saviour
From this soul of mine must pour
The desire to know Him better
And the longing for much more!*

*Not as one without possession
But having little, to desire
The embers stirred and fanned
Into a flaming fire!*

*Not 'til I stand before Him
For Whom my soul has cried
Will the yearning in me cease
And be fully satisfied!*

## Broken Pieces

*Has everything fallen apart
In all the things that mattered?
Then bring Me the broken pieces
That at your feet lie shattered.*

*All your dreams and high ambitions -
All your plans that went awry -
Now pieces that will not fit
No matter how hard you try.*

*How did everything come unglued?
It matters not how or when -
Bring Me the broken pieces,
And I'll fit them together again!*

*Look not at the shattered bits
But look full in My wonderful face,
And I'll gather up the pieces
And put them all in place!*

## Do You Wonder?

*Do you wonder why God's taken
Someone dear away from you
And left an ache deep in your heart
In spite of all you do?*

*Do you wonder why as days go by
Even God seems not to care,
Until the cross He's given you
Seems almost too great to bear?*

*Do you wonder why the days seem long
And nights seem not to end,
And your crushed and broken heart
Will never seem to mend?*

*Do you wonder why the gap that's left
Grows wider day by day,
And no other one can seem to fill
It quite the same old way?*

*God has left that gap on purpose
That He might dwell therein
And make Himself more precious
Than He has ever been!*

*Just as wounds are drawn together
When healing ointment is applied,
So Christ will fill that place
Now empty at your side.*

*He'll come with soothing balm -  
His healing you will feel,  
And though you'll bear the scar,  
Your broken heart will heal.*

*Yes, friend, He'll fill that void -  
That very lonely place -  
With His tender, loving comfort  
And His all-sufficient grace!*

# First Love

*Oh, give back to me, Father,
That warm and vibrant glow
That filled each day with sunlight
From the love I used to know!*

*When the wonder of Thy grace
Made my heart to overflow
And my days a heav'n on earth
Because I loved Thee so!*

*When Thou alone were first
And nothing seemed to hide Thee -
When Thou were all in all
And there was none beside Thee.*

*Oh, fill again my heart,
For this my prayer shall be -
May I fall in love, dear Lord,
All over again with Thee!*

## Another Christmas

*I hung a little angel
Upon the Christmas tree
And thought of how real angels
Will some day welcome me!*

*I hung the tiny lights
And watched with pure delight
As they twinkled and they sparkled
And brightened up the night!*

*And I thought of all the light
That I will someday see
When I hear my Saviour say,
I want you home, my child, with Me!*

*I hung a glittering star
and thought how wonderful to be
At home above for Christmas -
The Bright and Morning Star to see!*

*I draped the tree with garland
And visualized the sight
Of being there for Christmas
Dressed in a robe of white!*

*I placed the manger scene
Beneath the Christmas tree
And marvelled at the gift
Of love He gave to me!*

*And I couldn't help but think
Of grateful tears I ought to shed
For each Christmas that He gave me
And those in glory yet ahead!*

## He Cares

*Unseen, yet always there,
Someone watches you -
Never leaves your side
The whole day through.*

*Surely you must feel Him -
His presence is so real,
He, the great Physician,
Abundantly able to heal!*

*Standing there beside you
To hear your faintest cry -
His grace  so all-sufficient
Each day that passes by.*

*Oh, dear friend, look up
To the One beside you there
And hear those precious words,
I still answer prayer!*

## I'll Be Waiting

*T*hough on earth we say farewell,
This is my earnest prayer -
To say hello in heaven
And all its glories share!

To part would bring me pain,
But ne'er could it compare
To walking streets of gold
And finding you not there.

All through our separation
Your arrival I'll await,
And eagerly I'll look for you
And watch at heaven's gate.

I cannot leave you wealth -
My wealth is up above,
But I leave you something precious -
Christ's legacy of love.

Because I love you dearly
And you're all the world to me,
I want us all together
Throughout eternity!

## His Hands

*Unclean, Unclean! the leper screamed,*
*And those who heard his cry*
*Knew well its tragic meaning*
*And stood back to let him by.*

*'Twas only One who did not mind*
*How near the leper came,*
*But touched him with a healing hand,*
*Yes, Jesus was His name!*

*The blind, the lame, the suffering -*
*Ask them what they thought*
*Of those dear loving hands of His*
*And how much joy they brought.*

*Many a mother's little child*
*Knew the gentle tenderness*
*Of those dear hands upon his head*
*In gentle, sweet caress.*

*Oh, hands that ever sought*
*To ease man's misery*
*Have they taken in their wickedness*
*And bound so painfully.*

*And men today are binding*
*His hands unwittingly*
*In their constant, firm rejection*
*Of the Man of Calvary.*

*Oh, soul without a Saviour,*
*Will you keep bound by sin*
*Those hands that bore such agony,*
*Your redemption thus to win?*

❦

## I Care

*Dear friend, I know that you're hurting,*
*Although you never will say,*
*I know by the tone of your voice*
*That you live with your loss every day!*

*The tears that spring to your eyes -*
*Unbidden, yet suddenly there,*
*Dear friend, they go not unnoticed -*
*I want you to know that I care!*

*That longing to see your beloved -*
*Still undiminished by time,*
*I put myself in your place*
*And I care - your heartache is mine!*

❦

## Arrival

*Think of my coming home
To a beautiful, glorious place -
Think of me never in darkness
But warmed by the light of His face!*

*Think of me gazing in wonder
At Him, always there to behold,
Think of me taking His hand
And walking down streets of pure gold!*

*Think of me meeting with loved ones
I've missed so much through the years,
And think of the joyful reunion
That now replaces my tears!*

*Think of me talking to Spurgeon,
To the prophets and Moody and Paul -
Think of the rich fellowship
And the delight of meeting them all!*

*Think of me joining the angels
In glorious, triumphant song -
Think of me constantly singing
Praises to God the day long!*

*Think of Him making so plain
All the things I'd not understood,
And think of Him showing how all
Had worked together for good!*

*So think of me not as departing -
I've left just a shell of no worth,
But think of my happy arrival
And a joy unknown on earth!*

# His Star of Gold

*Oh, broken-hearted mother,*
*Why do you doubt My love?*
*Did I not also have a star*
*Of blue up here above?*

*And did I not know heartache*
*When I saw my star of blue*
*Turn to gold when on a cross*
*I let Him give His life for you?*

*Perhaps just now you'll know*
*The price I paid for you -*
*My star I turned to gold*
*When I could have kept it blue.*

*Oh, do not harbor bitterness*
*Nor let your heart grow cold -*
*Some day you'll understand*
*Why I turned your star to gold.*

*Oh, look beyond - and up!*
*Behold what shines for you!*
*On earth your star is gold -*
*In heaven it's still blue!*

## Possessions

*"Cisterns that hold no water" -*
*Oh Lord, how very true -*
*Possessions here on earth*
*Cannot satisfy like you!*

*For everything that is without*
*Will pass away some day,*
*But that which is within my heart*
*No man can take away.*

*Health and other losses*
*Often make the smooth path rough,*
*But oh, the precious thought -*
*Having Thee, I have enough!*

*The possession of earthly things -*
*May it never be my goal,*
*May I want to own none other*
*Than the owner of my soul!*

## The Master Potter

*I fought so hard against His will -*
*My troubled heart would not be still;*
*Bitter, bitter pangs within*
*Where once before peace had been.*
*I could not, would not, understand*
*This working of my Father's hand,*
*And further from His face I turned*
*And more and more His love I spurned.*
*And then I remembered one glad day*
*That He is the Potter, I but the clay;*
*'Twas not for me to question the mold*
*The master Potter would unfold.*
*Oh, He who loves this soul of mine,*
*Does He not know the right design?*

## My Message

*My words were so simple,
My voice wasn't strong,
And the message itself
Was not very long.*

*I know that I stammered
As I looked at a sea
Of faces that seemed
To be glued upon me.*

*And I wished at the time
Someone else in my place
Whose finer outline
My listeners could trace.*

*But it seemed as I stood there,
A voice hushed and stilled
Whispered to fear not,
My mouth would be filled.*

*And then I remembered -
My words were not mine -
I was only a channel
For my Master divine.*

*I wasn't up there
To be heard or be seen -
Just His voice through a vessel
Yielded and clean!*

## My Prayer

*God forgive
When I fail to get alone with Thee,
When I'm not the Christian I ought to be,
When dying souls I do not see -
Dear God, forgive!*

*God forgive
When I walk in my own selfish way,
When Thy precious words I don't obey,
When I don't draw closer every day -
Dear God, forgive!*

*God forgive
When my tongue has said a bitter thing,
When Thy praises I often fail to sing,
When I've not sought refuge 'neath Thy wing -
Dear God, forgive!*

## My Resurrection Day

When the time of parting comes,
Though your eyes with tears be dim,
Remember, I'll be happy,
For I'll be at last with Him!

When my spirit takes its leave,
And to heaven it has flown,
I'll have a brand new body
Fashioned like His own!

Mourn not a little plot of ground -
I won't be there - ah no,
I'll be walking with my Saviour,
And greater joy I'll never know.

So shed no tears of sadness
When I have gone away,
For it will be for me
My Resurrection Day!

# The Other Chapel

*Dear Lord, I love your house,*
*You know that this is true -*
*The songs of praise - the preaching,*
*My certain favorite pew.*

*But there's another chapel*
*To which I often flee -*
*It's still and quiet there,*
*Meant alone for You and me!*

*No one else attends this chapel -*
*I'm alone its single guest,*
*But it's here that I have found*
*My soul's at peace and rest.*

*Sins confessed, forgiven -*
*Communion again restored,*
*And the troubled waters stilled*
*In this chapel with my Lord.*

*You alone have all my worship -*
*Other gods cannot be mine,*
*For in this private chapel*
*There can be no other shrine.*

*Just You and I, dear Lord,*
*Communing with each other,*
*And my eyes on You alone*
*And not upon another.*

*With all life's earthly stress,*
*What delight to come apart*
*And worship Thee, my Saviour,*
*In the chapel of my heart!*

## Troubled Waters

*Let Him walk upon the waters*
*Of all your troubles, friend -*
*See Him calm the raging storm*
*And bring it to an end.*

*Be not afraid, He whispers -*
*I will calm your troubled sea -*
*Look not at the rolling waves,*
*Just look, dear one, at Me.*

*I'll take your hand in mine -*
*The fearful storm will pass,*
*I'll whisper, Peace be still,*
*And your sea will be as glass.*

*The troubled waters won't engulf -*
*He'll make the stormy winds a sigh,*
*Oh, sweet words of Christ -*
*Fear not, for it is I!*

# Unrest

*Oh Lord, what anxious days
Have come to our fair land -
What unrest sweeps across
This universe You planned.*

*Men's hearts today are troubled
More than ever, it would seem,
And the lasting peace they hope for
Now only seems a dream.*

*My hope lies in your promise -
What a comfort 'tis to me -
"Thou will keep him in perfect peace
Whose mind is stayed on Thee!"*

## Only Leaves

*There must be sadness in His eyes,
And I'm sure the Saviour grieves
When He looks in vain for fruit
And finds there only leaves!*

*Oh, how patiently He waits -
Tenderly granting reprieves,
And still no fruit appears -
Nothing - nothing but leaves!*

*There's an emptiness, alas,
The Christian heart perceives
In bearing fruitless branches
And only abundance of leaves!*

*For within his heart he knows
Satisfaction he retrieves
When his life is bearing fruit
And more than just the leaves.*

*Through every fleeting day
Into his heart there weaves
The Saviour's gentle wooing -
"Show me fruit, not just the leaves!"*

## The Ladder Beside You

*Do you sometimes feel like Jacob,*
*Your head on a pillow of stone,*
*With the night closing in around you*
*And feeling so very alone?*

*Ah, friend, remember the ladder*
*The Lord has put by your place,*
*Its foot right there beside you -*
*At the top His radiant face!*

*Oh, grasp tightly the ladder -*
*Look up and follow the light,*
*He'll ever be there waiting*
*And not lose you from His sight.*

*He'll see each faltering step*
*And eyes with tears that brim*
*And reach down to firmly grasp*
*That hand you lift to Him!*

*Each step will bring you closer,*
*His form you'll clearly trace,*
*As the darkness disappears -*
*In its place, His warm embrace!*

## How Much Time for Me?

*You were so occupied today -*
*Engaged so busily,*
*But answer this, my child,*
*How much time was given Me?*

*Oh yes, your tasks were much worthwhile,*
*Of that I quite agree,*
*But they took all your day -*
*How much was given Me?*

*You've talked to friends in number*
*And quite devotedly,*
*But here the day has gone,*
*And what was said to Me?*

*How can you say you love me*
*When earth's cares so vividly*
*Require your whole attention*
*And there is no time for Me?*

*Oh, precious child of mine,*
*How I long to make you see*
*That to get to know me better*
*You must get alone with Me!*

## Not Without Him

*I could sooner do without the sun,*
*The moon, or stars that shine -*
*I could sooner do without them all*
*Than have Thee not as mine!*

*I could sooner do without the joy*
*Of eyes with which to see*
*Than have Thee not as Saviour*
*And know your love for me!*

*I could sooner do without the joy*
*Of ears that hear each sound*
*Than do without the precious love*
*That I in Thee have found!*

*I could sooner do without my feet*
*And hands, oh yes, it's true,*
*Than having not the peace within*
*That comes alone from You!*

*I could sooner do without the air*
*I breathe, in truth I say,*
*Than live without Thee, Lord,*
*A single moment of each day!*

## Just a Pilgrim

*Oh, how endless seems my walk,
And I wish I'd hear Him say,
"You've walked so far and are so weary -
Come on home with Me today!"*

*Oh, the heartaches and the burdens
That His presence would erase,
Oh, the warmth my soul would know
From the sunshine of His face!*

*Yes, I get a longing to go home
And to see the One whose love
Makes my heart on earth so restless
'Til it rests with Him above.*

*Still a pilgrim down on earth
With a longing all the time
For the open arms of Jesus
And the home I know is mine!*

## Perfect Peace

*They laugh and sing, seem light of heart,*
*Do they my peace possess?*
*Ah, no, deep down within*
*There lies an emptiness.*

*Like the ashes from a fire*
*There lies smouldering within*
*The reeking of a burned-up life*
*And unforgiven sin.*

*Ever in mirth, a heaviness*
*In a heart that yearns for rest,*
*Like a stranger seeking haven*
*On some unknown quest.*

*Oh, Christian, thank your Saviour*
*For the peace that floods your soul,*
*And thank Him for the fullness*
*Of a life in His control!*

# Full of Joy

*Thou shalt make me full of joy?*
*But Lord, I look around*
*And find the things that vex me*
*And my joy does not abound.*

*Make me full of joy?*
*When conditions aren't the best*
*And prayers seemingly unanswered*
*Give my spirit little rest?*

*Make me full of joy?*
*Oh Lord, how can it be*
*When I know that often others*
*Do not see you lived through me.*

*Ah, the secret You have given*
*As I read on in Thy Word -*
*And cold embers start to glow*
*As my heart is warmed and stirred.*

*I've looked within, without,*
*And not the upward gaze*
*Upon Thy lovely countenance*
*That warms like sunlit rays.*

*How simple - yet so true,*
*How often I fail to see*
*That full of joy I'll surely be*
*When I find my joy in Thee!*

# The Stranger

*I slip into your church
A stranger, unaware -
So quietly you do not know
That I am sitting there.*

*And I watch you Christians closely
And observe your every way -
I listen as you testify
And as you sing and pray.*

*I feel the peace and quiet
Of the reverent atmosphere,
And it seems that God Himself
Must be standing very near.*

*And something grips my heart
I cannot quite explain -
Here is life and peace and joy
In the message you proclaim.*

*Here is worship from the heart -
How great this One must be
Who, though unseen by you,
Is loved so obviously.*

*Yes, I watch you Christians closely
Until the meeting's through,
And then accept your Saviour
Because of what He means to YOU!*

# WMBI

*I had a dream the other night -
T'was really quite a nightmare,
I dreamed I dialed Moody's
And the station wasn't there!*

*How could this be, I wondered -
It's been on for years and years,
As furiously I dialed
Amidst new mounting fears.*

*There were many other stations
With loud commercial pitches,
But not the station proclaiming
The Lord's eternal riches.*

*No Bible study or sermons -
No hymns of inspiration -
How could I have taken for granted
My beloved radio station?*

*The sound of the alarm
Brought back reality
And a new appreciation
For what Moody's meant to me.*

*With untold joy I heard
Greeting his radio flock
The welcome voice of Murfin
On good old "Morning Clock."*

*On through the day I listened
And offered a grateful prayer
That I had only been dreaming -
The Moody network was still there!*

## The Adversary

*Tired and worn one evening,*
*I did not stop to pray -*
*T'was in the stillness of the night*
*I seemed to hear one say.....*

*If I can rob a Christian*
*Of time alone with Him,*
*I can cause his feet to stumble*
*While his Master's face grows dim.*

*If I can rob a Christian*
*Of time spent with His Word,*
*I can get his mind to doubting*
*While his Saviour's face is blurred.*

*Excuses by the hundreds*
*Will I whisper in his ear*
*And break the sweet communion*
*With the One he holds so dear.*

*Yes, I can break their fellowship*
*And make him cease to care,*
*Just by cheating him of precious time*
*Down on his knees in prayer.*

*There is alone a moment*
*That I cannot gain a place,*
*And that is when a Christian*
*Is gazing in His face!*

*I could not listen longer -*
*My eyes with tears were dim,*
*And e'er I fell asleep*
*I had talked alone with Him!*

## A Teacher's Prayer

*As I stood and gazed one morning*
*At each little empty chair,*
*I could not help but bow my head*
*And breathe this earnest prayer.*

*Oh, God, my heavenly Father,*
*Make me never satisfied*
*Until I see my little class*
*As souls for whom Thou died.*

*Help me go before my class*
*With this one solemn aim -*
*That these dear little ones*
*May bring glory to Thy name!*

*If in only one young life*
*Thou had blotted out sin's stain,*
*T'would make my heart rejoice and know*
*My work was not in vain.*

*They are with me but an hour,
But e'er its minutes flee,
May precious souls be reached
For all eternity!*

*May I never see just children
Who listen to my voice,
But lives whom I can influence
To make my Lord their choice!*

## God's Hand

*Two sons God gave to me,*
*Gifts of love unmeasured,*
*When death stepped in and claimed*
*One of the two I treasured.*

*When death unclasped my hands*
*From those of my dear son,*
*'Twas then I felt God's hand*
*Closing 'round my empty one!*

*And a peace I never knew*
*Nor yet could understand*
*Flowed through my grieving heart*
*With the pressure of His hand.*

*I knew He'd share my sorrow -*
*That emptiness He'd fill*
*With His hand upon my own*
*To quiet and to still.*

*Not a teardrop falls unbidden -*
*Not a whisper of a moan,*
*But I feel His hand grow tighter,*
*Clasped around my own!*

## He Was There

*Home at last, I sighed,
How good it looked to me -
For days it was the only place
I really wanted to be.*

*Home from painful surgery -
Pain not easily endured,
Now all at last behind me
And I was finally cured.*

*And then - just hours later -
Eight to be exact,
Pain began again,
And I faced a cruel fact.*

*The pain wasn't going away,
Try as I would to will it,
And a nagging inner voice
Whispered nothing was going to still it.*

*Dear Lord, I cried in anguish,
Have I not endured enough?
I've tried to be submissive,
But this is really rough!*

*If you really loved me, Lord,
You could heal me right away
And take away the pain
Without a moment's delay.*

*But back to the hospital again -*
*Had He not heard my cry?*
*And through an avalanche of tears*
*I could only question why.*

*Ah, but then a sweet, sweet peace*
*Which comes only from above*
*Settled 'round about me*
*Like the landing of a dove.*

*And I felt the prayers of loved ones*
*Wafting up on loving wings*
*To give me calm assurance*
*Of the healing Jesus brings.*

*And once again I learned*
*That no matter what the test*
*The Lord is in control*
*And His way is always best!*

*From beginning to the end*
*Through a cloudy, misty hall,*
*He never left my side -*
*He was there throughout it all!*

## Bookworm

*The closet filled with books*
*Belonging to the master*
*Could only be described*
*As the scene of a disaster!*

*There were books on the shelves,*
*There were books on the floor,*
*And the bookworm kept adding*
*And adding some more!*

*Some day I am sure*
*When I open the door,*
*The books will pour out*
*And I'll land on the floor!*

*Oh, well, it is hopeless -*
*I'll forget how it looks,*
*For I know he won't stop*
*From adding more books.*

*And when he adds enough books*
*For a library branch,*
*I'm sure he'll be buried*
*In a book avalanche!*

*And his tombstone will read -*
*He added ONE MORE*
*And made the mistake*
*Of opening the door!*

# Not Easy Being Green

*Old Doc was looking worried -*
*This is mighty strange, my dear,*
*For I do perceive you have*
*Something GREEN within your ear!*

*Nurse! Quickly! Get my forceps!*
*And make it on the double -*
*This dear old lady here*
*Is in a heap of trouble!*

*Ah, there, I have it out*
*And sure enough, it's GREEN!*
*In all my years of practice*
*This sight I've never seen!*

*This alarming specimen*
*Must be studied in detail*
*And a cure at once be found*
*Or it's the end of Martindale!*

*Well, by now the green-eared patient,*
*More worried by the minute,*
*Wondered why her ear had held*
*This alarming green within it!*

*The doctor looked so worried -*
*Was she doomed or was there hope?*
*Those forceps with the green*
*Made it difficult to cope.*

*Ah, but doomed she would not be -
The answer made her fairly sing -
Dear doctor, I must tell you -
I washed with good old Irish Spring!*

*Old Doc was mortified -
Medical mystery of the year,
Just residue - GREEN SOAP
Left in the patient's ear!*

*He did a hasty retreat
Mumbling words one should not hear
About his weirdo patient
With GREEN SOAP still in her ear!*

# My Jim

*When you were born
You never knew
The love I felt
When I saw YOU!*

*So perfectly formed -
An eight-pound boy!
You never knew
Your mother's joy!*

*And you never knew
As I watched you grow
How terribly much
I loved you so!*

*Born second, to be sure,
I cannot change that part,
But NEVER, my dear Jim,
Were you second in my heart!*

## Father's Songs

Many years have come and gone
But I still hear the ring
Of songs I heard so often -
The hymns my father used to sing.

"I walk with the King, hallelujah:"
Oh, how many were the days
I heard his happy voice
As he sang that hymn of praise!

Yes, my father loved the Lord
And knew His saving grace,
And I know his joy was full
When he met Him face to face.

Some day when Jesus calls me
To join that heavenly throng,
I'll see my precious father
And join him in his song!

# A Rival

*Keep the television low
And hold those blasted phones -
For Martindale is reading
None other than LLOYD-JONES!*

*Please - a word of caution -
Speak in whispered tones,
For the Reverend is absorbed
In a volume by LLOYD-JONES!*

*A visitor approaching?
How the master groans,
For he'd rather be alone
With a copy of LLOYD-JONES!*

*And if you listen closely
You'll hear the tragic moans
Of a wife who's been deserted
For the books of old LLOYD-JONES!*

## A Mother's Crusade

*Each bookstore is a challenge,
Be it large or be it small -
To the mother of an author,
It matters not at all.*

*She bolts into each store
In a never-ending raid
To see that management
Keeps her author's book displayed!*

*Shelves are scanned in earnest
For the ONE book on her mind,
And woe be unto the store
If son's book she cannot find!*

*Rounding up the manager,
She demands an explanation
As to why they haven't stocked
The best book in the nation!*

*And if the book is there
(As it surely ought to be),
She sees that it's arranged
For every eye to see.*

*It can't be tucked away -
It must be right in front -
Where each prospective buyer
Its title will confront.*

*Like a mother hen she hovers
In front of the window display
And searches for that cover
That would really make her day!*

*But alas, it's never there -
Worthless books take up the space,
While the one of greatest value
Hasn't gained a window space!*

*Oh well, the author's brilliant -
His best seller's yet to come,
And Mama can stop promoting
When his book is NUMBER ONE!*

## Cloud of Grief

*The sky had seemed so clear -
A wide expanse of blue,
And then, no bigger than a hand,
A cloud came into view.*

*'Tis only just a cloud,
It will dissipate, I said,
My son is very ill
But better days are yet ahead.*

*But the cloud grew larger, darker
And hung heavy in the sky,
And my heart began to fear
That my son might even die!*

*And then the dark cloud broke,
Raining down such awful sorrow
That I cared not if I lived
To see one more tomorrow!*

*And in its aftermath
How oft my heart has cried,
Dear Lord, he was so young -
It was I who should have died!*

*Since first that cloud appeared
On that happy cloudless day,
My heart just keeps on breaking,
And tears are never far away!*

## Still Flying

*From my hospital room I look
Into the brilliant sky
And watch as one by one
The planes go passing by.*

*And a dream impossible -
But so badly do I want it -
That the plane out there would have
My dearest David on it!*

*Why is it still so difficult
Watching the planes out there
And knowing he will never land
Again at our O'Hare?*

*And then my mind recalls
All the times I saw and heard
The planes he DID come on -
Sweeter sound than any bird!*

*Even now, dear son of mine,
'Til the day that I am dying,
It's not just another plane -
You're still up there - FLYING!*

## Heavenly Passport

*It really doesn't matter*
*How long my earth's duration,*
*For I'm bound for another land,*
*And I have a reservation.*

*I made it years ago*
*When at the cross one day*
*I acknowledged Christ as Saviour*
*And He washed my sins away!*

*And my name was written down -*
*Eternally recorded -*
*And a place reserved for me*
*'Til death's waters I have forded.*

*When I take that final trip,*
*Then I, like other mortals,*
*Must have a valid passport*
*To enter heaven's portals.*

*And when I stand before Him,*
*It's not good works for which He'll look,*
*But whether I've a reservation*
*And my name is in His book!*

# Waiting Room

*I'm just waiting in the lobby
For the sound of angel wing
To escort me to the throne room
And the presence of the King.*

*I do not know how long the wait,
Whether it be short or long,
Before the door is opened
To the sound of heaven's song.*

*The vestibule is lovely
But it's just a waiting place
'Til the throne room door is opened
And I see Him face to face!*

*So with eager expectation
I look beyond the hall
To the rooms that He will open
When my name His angels call.*

*From this waiting room I'll go
To rooms so full of light
And to such awesome splendor
I'll scarce contain the sight!*

*Today I can only see
The light beneath the door,
But some day that door will open
And I'll wait in the hall no more!*

Other books by FOCUS PUBLISHING

**The Perilous Quest**
Book One - *The Legend of Garison Fitch*
Book Two - *Lost Time**
Book Three - *Saving Time**

Joan Cooks **"Heart Smart Cooking"**

**Mysteries of the New Testament**

**Space Bender***

*\*Forthcoming*

20-23
25,